1000 PROVERBS

S. J. FOWLER
&
TOM JENKS

NEWTON-LE-WILLOWS

Published in the United Kingdom in 2015.
by The Knives Forks And Spoons Press,
122 Birley Street,
Newton-le-Willows,
Merseyside,
WA12 9UN.

ISBN 978-1-909443-59-4

Copyright © Steven Fowler & Tom Jenks, 2015.

The right of Steven Fowler & Tom Jenks to be identified as the author of this work has been asserted by them in accordance with the Copyrights, Designs and Patents Act of 1988. All rights reserved. No part of this publication may be reproduced, stored in a retrieval system, transmitted in any form or by any means, electronic, photocopying, recording or otherwise, without prior permission of the publisher.

Acknowledgements:

The cover image shows Theo Kaccoufa's Squid Bear, 2001, polyester resin, aluminium foil, aluminium paint, 40 x 24 x 23 cm.

1000 PROVERBS

Corn grows well in a small field.

The sluggard ploughs in carpet slippers.

The headless army can be in for a hard time.

The hat burns on the head of the arsonist.

The healthy racist doesn't need a watch.

A leopard is a joy forever.

Even the crow sings with its own voice.

A talkative bird is a casserole.

Everyone carries his own skins to the market.

Even a bear can be taught to whistle.

Until a bear has smoked out the bees, he can't eat the honey.

The prudent man spreads marmalade.

When bears fight, it is the grass that suffers.

A bear is just a man in a suit.

Bite not the nut that bites.

In the valley of the monkeys, the peanut vendor is king.

Monkeys are small but strong.

A chimpanzee has no need of a razor.

You can walk a dog to death if you get permission from its owner.

A man who chases two dogs is committing an offence.

A lunatic who always enjoys his meals will never regain understanding.

Never coddle an egg for a madman.

A little sheep always seems young.

One man's shorts are another man's hot pants.

He is one pamphlet behind the others.

He is one hand short of a shandy.

He puts his sickle into another man's harvest.

A cat may look at a King, but a mole requires contact lenses.

To a skinny cat, all the world is a flea.

If you lie down with dogs, you will always get a bone.

A big man with no intellect is a log.

Speak softly and carry a Dictaphone.

A man who studies experimental poetry will not get funding.

A life without poetry is chicken nuggets.

A woman and a melon are hard to choose.

At the self-service checkout, a melon is a problem.

If melons are hid for winter, the spring can expect seeds.

If life gives you lemons, become a greengrocer.

A lemon is only sour to the mouth that eats it.

A lemon in the hand is worth 49 pence.

An old ape never made a pretty smile.

You can't teach an old ape social networking.

An ape on a ship is a sick ape.

A sick ape shuns even the smallest banana.

A man who loves a fox enters heaven red.

Croutons lead the fox to the salad station.

Not for nothing does the salad have a sneeze guard.

A man who never sneezes knows not ecstasy.

A dirty mouth will never stay clean.

The sharpest tongue does not slice a lettuce.

A slug without a lettuce is blind to a bank note.

To a snail, a slug is a nudist.

A Dutch slug is orange but once a year.

Never trust a Dutchman with your elms.

A Dutch oven is never cold in winter.

You'll never own the waterworks with your finger in the dyke.

You'll never own a dyke in Holland.

You will never be as lonely as a famous Belgian.

Bargains are costly.

It is cheaper to go by foot than invent a horse.

A daft nurse makes a wise wean.

A wise nurse never touches the equipment.

A good nurse never blames her tools.

No-one remembers the inventor of the bum bag.

There will be no peace until pasta.

Today's spaghetti is tomorrow's shoelace.

Be patient with a bad neighbour, he may move or have some bad luck.

Give a man a fish and you have fed him for today. Teach a man to fish and you have given him a hobby.

The sausage duvet unfurling is a hazard to many a sleeping man.

A sausage gives a dog vocabulary.

The birthday treat lasts but a day.

Only a pedant spellchecks a birthday cake.

A candle is not a cat.

A cat in a warehouse is worth two in a call centre.

A primarch is a leader of men.

A grown man should not weep in Primark.

A red jacket does not make you a racer.

A tartan shopping trolley is not a disability.

The wheels of the bus go round and round.

There is no malady that cannot be cured by murder.

Only a chimp's tit can twist the lips of a jungle sickness.

You cannot contract malaria in Eccles.

An Eccles cake is hardly a cake.

You can make an eggless sponge without breaking eggs.

A sponge is the hand is a sponge in the bath.

A gentleman does not share his bath or his diseases.

A gentleman is a man who would never hit a woman with his glasses on.

A gentleman's best friend is his relish.

Education begins a gentleman, poetry completes him.

To the gentleman, poetry is as essential as musk.

A Canadian pharmacy is never understocked.

A horse cannot join the mounted police.

A flap of skin need not always be sewn.

A stitch in time saves an otter's pocket.

A clown's pocket is full of tricks.

Never offer to clean a clown's shoes.

A clown is like a bubble, one prick and it's gone.

Never pass wind in a bubble car.

Never wind a car in a bubble.

In a hearse, there are no back seat drivers.

Sometimes medicine tastes bad, but you have to swallow it.

The bitterest pill tastes nice with cider.

No man is River Island.

There is no point shoplifting in Aldi.

Tesco Value is always valued.

We are all as individual as individual fruit pies.

Eating a pie from McDonalds is like going to a butcher's for a prostitute.

There is nothing more satisfying than a sausage.

Don't trust a man inviting you to swim in his bath.

Never trust a man who shares his loofah.

Never wash in a public toilet.

You can take a horse to the toilet, but only in Cumbria.

Don't eat cheese in a hot spring.

As a lady has wiles, so the Swiss have innumerable cheeses.

A Romanian lady need not be feared.

There is always a man in Romania.

There are mountains in the Ukraine.

Never show a chicken a map of Kiev.

To have egg on your face is not nice.

Don't put all of your eggs in a rucksack.

Don't put all your eggs in one bastard.

Better an egg today than an egg nog tomorrow.

Better Butlin's than a Russian prison.

Better a scarf in Skegness than rubber gloves in Minehead.

Better a wrestler in the vale than in Bognor Regis.

Better a bugger in Bognor than a penis in Penistone.

Better buggered in Athens than in Sparta.

Even the Greek gods smash their plates.

Nyan nyan nyan nyan nyan nyan nyan nyan nyan nyan nyan nyan nyan nyan.

There is nothing more dramatic than a chipmunk.

This is madness. Madness? This is Sparta.

Even green fingers do not belong in salad.

A salad a day to world peace beckoning.

French dressing does not make you a musketeer.

Muskets are not just for the mustard.

A musket in public, a blunderbuss in private.

A bus to school, a taxi to the hospital.

There are no IT lessons in a school of whales.

The beluga whale is whiter than a Band-Aid.

You can't get caviar from a surgeon.

A fox on a trampoline is a garden delight.

The most cunning fox is not a magician.

A magician tickles the hand in order to distract the rabbit.

When a wizard attends a fancy dress party, he must expect to have his beard pulled.

When ape technique, o my god wrestling.

Do not wrestle with an ape, except in jest.

A baby bison is not a cat's paw.

When a cat wears gloves, the violin is impossible.

To fall in love with the violin is a hurt for the liver.

A horn section should not give a solo recital.

The horn of jorumun was built in segments.

The horn of plenty is illegal after 9pm.

The horn of mead is a fantasy trope.

You can't dissolve a monastery in a glass of water.

An egg won't boil inside a chicken.

A chicken has no concept of goujons.

The swede is a nation from the soil.

Dick Turnip was not a highwayman.

Paraguay is not a country.

There's more to Brazil than Brazilians.

The new trailer for Prometheus is mind-blowing.

You cannot keep an eagle in a caravan.

A mobile home is not a home.

Never split an atom in a two man tent.

A sausage skin is made to split.

There's more to a sausage than sausage meat.

There's more to Spain than sausage.

Cheese without pickle is like cheese without pickle.

Don't get too close to a pickle, it will betray you.

A fool and his onions are soon pickled.

A merry fool is a ready victim.

An idiot is eloquent when he enters parliament.

A bee is still a bee when a bee is a bead.

A beard is a beard except when it's a moustache.

A man under the age of thirty who has a beard is the Yorkshire ripper.

They don't wear tartan at Scotland Yard.

If you hear cheese in the Police station, cover your penis.

There is no such thing as an ironic "truncheon".

An ironic truncheon is like a speedboat; it's meant to mean something.

A canoe without a paddle is like a duck without feet.

A duck without feet is like a canoe without an engine.

A duck without luck is an unlucky duck.

A duck without feet is a meal fit for the Chinese.

Never judge a book by its bookmark.

I lost my bookmark in the riots.

Happiness is a fully healed rotator cuff injury.

No man wants to go to prison.

Not all men can consort with Croats.

A saying is a flower; a proverb is a berry flavoured protein shake.

In London, mushy peas are guacamole.

In Manchester, a hot pot is all that is left over.

Betty Turpin did not rob stagecoaches.

A Megabus is better than a stagecoach.

A double decker has no drawing room.

A Double Decker is no Spira.

You can't play it straight on a bendy bus.

You can't bend a straight bus.

You can bend a straight man if he's flexible.

It takes two men to bend a bow.

They didn't listen to *The Archers* at Agincourt.

The baby monkey is wrapped around the mother monkey.

Inside every monkey is an organ grinder.

Inside every organ is a grinding monkey.

You don't need to buy a bonobo dinner.

A bonobo knows how to have a good time.

A bonobo is too big for a cat flap.

A cat flap is not the kind of flap a bonobo seeks to enter.

The Archbishop of Canterbury does not believe in monkeys.

I don't remember a single line of *Red Dragon*.

If Burton is dead, turn to Hopkins.

If Tony becomes Dylan Thomas, turn down the volume.

There are no car chases in *Under Milk Wood*.

Milk comes from nipples.

A coconut gives milk, but never touch its hair.

To milk a cow one need only feed the glove.

You can take a bullock to a hillock but you can't make it camp.

A daughter without her mother's hump is some kind of luck.

A camel without a hump is a horse.

A camel without water is a horse.

A horse without water is hoarse.

A whore without water is dead of thirst.

A thirsty man has no patience with ice cubes.

A patient man has no problem with ice he didn't order.

A penguin does not need a dinner jacket.

A fur lined coat is not an otter.

Fur lined underpants does not a mammoth make.

Jeff Hilson is not a fur lined poem.

A furry poet needs no cloak.

A furry cloak needs no poet.

Sir Walter Raleigh did not wear a hoody.

Spice a potato and spare the child.

Show me the potato and I will show you the crisps.

True calamari is not short of legs.

A squid ring is not apt for a lady's finger.

December is too long to wait.

Waders in November means a hard winter.

A book in a box is not a book.

Never judge a box by its jack.

When a man misses his hat, you know he needs his hair.

A bald man with a shaved head is still a bald man.

A fiery lemon is no friend to sunburn.

A crushed lime will make a warrior weep.

It's hip to be square.

The power of love is a curious thing.

Love makes one man weep, makes another man sing.

Love changeth a heart to a little white dove.

There are soundtracks to murder that one doesn't wish to hear too often.

Every man will one day be Brett Easton Ellis.

A woman with bacon in her hair is a Viking's wife.

The Pope cannot stomach a full English breakfast.

The Little Chef has big pancakes.

A drunken librarian will lose his appendix.

A doctor without a stethoscope is not a doctor.

A doctor without a white coat has nowhere to put his thermometer.

A northern doctor is an angel of mercy

An angel is a mathematician's misspelling.

A man of the ships shouldn't be trusted with a syringe.

A ship in a bottle has no duty free.

A ship in a bottle is a waste of a bottle

A plastic cork is impossible.

A man who loves Beethoven does not like to hear otherwise

Richard Wagner is not Robert Wagner.

When About the last night, sorry About that.

There is no garlic bread at the Last Night of the Proms.

Old garlic may be rubbery, but do not fear to eat it.

Never put all your chicken in a basket.

Never weave a basket of burning reeds.

Never lay an egg in another man's eggcup.

Never fill an eggcup with a chicken.

Never judge a chicken by its nuggets.

Never eat a nugget if you want to eat a chicken.

Never invite a lady to a boneless banquet.

Never serve fish at a dinner party.

Captain Birdseye doesn't eat crab sticks.

Crab sticks are not made of tears.

Never give a crab a sideways glance.

Never call lobster on a sleeping crab.

A lobster wearing mittens has no sense of self.

A man in a suit is ready to boil.

A man in a shell suit mocks the turtle.

The apple and the nut know the value of worms and shells.

One bad apple fouls the crumble.

A crumble is meant to come apart.

One man's crumble is another's broken biscuit.

Deja vu is a funny feeling in the legs.

You don't need a sock for a phantom limb.

A man with one leg is grateful for his arms.

A man without a care is deceased.

A dead man tells no lies.

A dead man tells no jokes.

A joke about a dead man is no lie.

Always wear underpants at funerals.

A translated poem is a like a funeral for ants.

Even an ant can't carry its own coffin.

A coffin without nails is safe practice.

A coffin without a lid is a surprise for everyone.

A paper coffin is no use at sea.

There's no point burying a mermaid at sea.

A mermaid is neither fish nor woman

A woman needs a fish like a man needs a bicycle.

A woman smells of fish when she rides a bicycle

An ironed fish is a flat fish.

If a man says a goldfish is a flatfish, he is a paedophile.

You cannot groom a goldfish.

A goldfish cannot be a highlander.

Scotland is not how it looks on biscuit tins.

Newquay is not a town for biscuits.

There is no nookie in Newquay.

There are no friends in a Cornish marriage

Try anything once except irony.

There are no liquids in an English breakfast

The British Empire was not built on yoghurt.

Too eager to leave is often quick to regret

Regrets are like sardines, except they don't come in tins.

A tinned fish is like a broken leg, it never really feels the same.

A fish with one fin moves in all the wrong circles.

A fish with three eyes is blind.

A fish without an eye is unpronounceable.

An eye without a patch is cold.

Pirates don't wear contact lenses.

A pirate with a parrot isn't much of a talker.

A pirate without a parrot hasn't read the job description.

A pirate is a parrot in a parallel universe.

Never ask a parrot to repeat itself.

Never ask a scouser what is dead

Never use the toilet on a Megabus.

David Bowie is not a friend to walls.

David Bowie cannot teach you bush craft.

The magic crystal is not a drug.

You don't need an aerial for a crystal ball.

You don't need Falkor for a never-ending story

A never-ending story is not suitable for bedtime.

A story that does not begin never ends.

Inside every romantic comedy, there is Jennifer Aniston trying to get out.

Jennifer Aniston does not work in Human Resources

You cannot coax Courtney Cox.

Friends are not Golden Girls.

Keep your friends close and your enemies in Worcester.

There is a sauce that has no source.

There will always be some inaccessible ketchup.

Ketchup is banned in France.

In England, French dressing is just for salads.

In France, English mustard is made from horse

A horse and a radish don't make horseradish.

A horse without a tail is like a chimp without teeth.

A chimp without teeth has no use for nuts.

If you tickle a chimp, be ready to lose your arm.

A fickle chimp will ride anyone's tricycle.

A fickle pickle is nobody's friend.

One man's cucumber is another's gherkin.

A cucumber is basically water.

A dehydrated cucumber spoils the buffet.

A broken condom spoils the mood

Coitus interruptus is not a martial art.

Egg foo young is a martial art.

You only need one syllable to name a panda.

A red panda is not a fired fox.

You can't fire a fox unless you employ it.

You can't douse a fire with hot piss.

You can't start a fire in a functioning urinal.

A chicken farm in Poland is not a University.

A chicken can't haunt you if it is not dead.

A barrow in furness is full of coal.

A radioactive sheep is not a nuclear deterrent.

Two Ph.D. students are not likely to save the world.

The world cannot be saved by a goalkeeper.

Samba is not only for the rich.

Zumba is not a race of people.

Do not get budget colonic irrigation.

Do not ask a haddock for a pedicure.

A rain of poems is not made of water.

A nun's umbrella is useless in heaven.

A forgotten habit is no use in the swimming pool.

There is no fun in a nunnery.

There ain't no soap in a funnery.

Don't put soap on the Pope.

Bulletproof glass shows everyone has doubts.

Never put a Cossack in a cassock.

A Cossack haircut is easily sunburnt.

You can't groom a Cossack with a Ladyshave.

Never shave a lamb in winter.

A wolf in sheep's clothing has psychological problems.

A wolf without teeth is a hat for hunters.

A wolf without teeth should become a counsellor.

The enemy of my friend is my enemy.

There is no enemy like a sea anemone.

Hitler had a busy life.

Better gerbils than Goebbels.

The human centipede is not a nice way to live.

Never offer to clean a centipede's shoes.

A centipede does not live inside a peach for free.

People who live in peaches shouldn't get stoned.

A man who talks to giant insects shouldn't criticise those who live in peaches.

A peach is a gift, but not under a pillow.

A pillow is a gift, but not over one's face.

A pillow down one's trousers is fun at the rectory.

Down the trousers runs the happy ferret.

A ferret in the hand is a bad idea.

A mink is not a ferret.

An escaped mink will not make a furry purse.

A marmot is mother to the mink, father to the ferret and cousin to the cat.

You can lead a man to Sussex with a mandatory break.

Mud in the eye is better than mud in the boot.

A poet in a tent makes an awning a wigwam.

A condom is a friend in a storm.

A punctured condom is no place for a tadpole.

A muddy field is no place for a worm.

A worm in a teapot is a surprise for the vicar.

The worm meets us all, eventually.

There is no point cracking jokes in a hearse.

A long black car might be a limousine.

A stretch limousine is no place for a jockey.

A jockey is a not a leprechaun.

A jockey without a horse is an admin error.

A night without toothpaste is achey.

There are no adventures with dentures.

It's hard to find a good dentist in prison.

A dentist in prison is Sir Laurence Olivier.

An actor need not really suffer.

A thespian should not have a lisp.

John Gielgud was part gibbon.

You'll never feel as good as Gielgud.

A Russian will not be hurried.

Inside every Russian is a doll.

Inside every red is a white.

You cannot unite a separated egg.

The egg is split in the grave.

Out of the frying pan, into the sandwich.

Too much broth not enough turnips.

A fly in the soup is waiting for a punchline.

A turnip is a frog's best friend come winter.

A mashed turnip is a terrible thing.

A Welsh underground is not a mine.

The Welsh underground does not wear berets.

Reading in Leeds is like reading to oneself.

Crossing the Pennines is best done metaphorically.

The penny has not dropped.

A penny in a pudding is inflationary.

A pudding is a bun in quarantine.

Never pour custard on a lady's trifle.

Never curdle custard creams.

You can still get indigestion from digestive biscuits.

An apple a day keeps you from needing to visit your local GP.

Never run in a walk-in centre.

Better ten times ill than one time dead.

A dead man needs no lozenges.

Dead men don't wear ties

Dead men don't read self-help books.

If a man can't help himself, I don't want nobody baby.

Baby vegetables make an insubstantial broth.

Baby elephants don't remember.

A Baby Bel is not born with rind.

You can't make an omelette without breaking legs.

You can make an omelette without breaking wind.

You can make the northern wind by shouting Chang!

The I Ching cannot distinguish your arse and elbow.

El buho is Spanish for owl.

A Spanish owl is lost in translation.

A buffalo cannot fly without man's hunger.

A buffalo without wings is useless in Nando's.

A fish without a head is like a bird without wings

You cannot catch a fillet o' fish.

You can't fillet a wisp.

The mildest man can batter a cod.

You lead a fish to water but you can't make it swim, if it is dead.

You can't catch a fish with a skinny maggot.

You can't step into the same river twice.

When Jesus walked on water, he wasn't wearing Wellingtons.

A sack full of Christ is no use when swimming.

A female version of Christ is a very naughty boy.

A female version of Christ is not the Virgin Mary.

There is no gold in Nescafé Gold Blend.

A sack full of gold is no use when swimming.

A sac half full is unfinished business.

A sack a half full is not a sack.

You won't find an egg in a spinster's rucksack.

The egg is mother to us all.

A hungry man shuns not a radish.

A radish is neither fruit nor foe, thus a man knows not what to do with it.

A bent banana is nothing to be ashamed of.

You must peel a banana before you freeze it

A strong pickled onion brooks no nonsense.

A devil's fruit has no place in the larder.

A devil on horseback has no place in dressage.

A gold in dressage is a medal worth winning if you're riding a gorilla.

A man who rides a gorilla should take precautions.

A gorilla who knows gold will not be content with silver.

A silverback gorilla doesn't need lucky underpants.

The king of the jungle doesn't need a crown.

The Lion King does not greet ambassadors.

The circle of life is square.

There is no excuse for Elton John.

If bitten by a werewolf, a man must accept his fate.

A man bitten by a werewolf needs more than a Ladyshave.

A man on his blog needs no meals.

A fool and his Blackberry are never parted.

A galaxy is too large to have sequels.

They didn't have seminars on the Death Star.

The death star is not a planet.

A princess for children, a Jedi for pleasure and a Wookie for ecstasy.

These are not the droids you're looking for.

You cannot moisturise an Ewok.

You cannot barbecue an Ewok when a Wookie is around.

A barbequed Ewok needs no marinade.

Too much salt is bad for bread.

Jesus always had enough left over for sandwiches.

Jesus wasn't built in a day.

The Holy Ghost doesn't trick or treat.

The Holy Spirit doesn't like the cold.

Better the Holy Spirit than holey underpants.

The Holier the water, the spicier the flavour

Holy water doesn't make nice Ribena.

Sugar free Ribena is not Ribena

There is no such thing as free sugar.

The body knows not sweet salt from sour sugar

One man's vinegar is another man's problem.

Women who love women are happy.

A cancelled event needs no publicity.

Charity begins at home.

Dogs should never play postman's knock.

A dog's dick is a butcher's friend.

A policeman's truncheon seldom brings pleasure.

A black pudding is red inside.

A black and white minstrel is not multiracial.

Two wrongs are really wrong.

Never keep your mistakes in jam jars.

Fool me once, fool on you, fool me twice, I'm not going to let you fool me again.

Only a fool performs their own vasectomy.

A monkey's muscle is good for lifting.

A monkey's uncle can't be trusted with your aunt.

A monkey nut is best kept shelled.

Never come between a monkey and its nuts.

Never chop a squid before you mash a pickle.

Cheese without pickle is an opportunity squandered.

A man running for office will punch you in the back.

You cannot run for office in a pair of winkle pickers.

A woman who chews her fingers can't give a massage.

A monkey puzzle tree has no solution.

Only the dead can know peace from this rustling.

Dead dogs mount no occasional tables.

There is no need to be upset.

An upset squirrel gathers no nuts.

Shhh, peace now, only dreams.

A man with a broken gutter drowns in his dreams.

None can rustle the triumvirate.

Julius Caesar did not invent the salad.

Dressing is not for punks.

You don't need a wardrobe to dress a salad.

You can't take a wardrobe on a robbery.

Robin Hood never laddered his tights.

The Korean Robin Hood lives Gangnam style.

Friar Tuck didn't bungee jump.

Friar Tuck was an atheist.

An atheist should keep out of the font.

There are plenty of atheists in foxholes.

A hungry fox has no scruples about giblets.

A fox in the night will fight with a cat.

The sleekest cat still makes a poor snood.

The Essex Lion always turns out a Maine Coon.

A lion in Essex is evenly tanned.

An evening tan is always brown.

Tan loafers do not a lounge lizard make.

Godzilla is not Godzuki.

You can't summon Godzilla with a farmer's whistle.

Mothra is a giant moth.

Giant moths make small curtains.

A curtain on fire is no shade from the sun.

One man's umbrella is another man's tee pee.

A yurt has no windows.

Yoghurt in a yurt confuses the lexicographer.

A horse in Mongolia is not for dinner

Ghengis Khan didn't use Just For Men.

Genghis Khan was not an only child

Kublai Khan did not smoke menthols.

The Tsar of Russia was a Viking Mongol.

Never give a Viking the horn.

Never attribute to malice that which is adequately explained by stupidity.

Never write someone else's suicide note.

A suicide note is best left unfinished

The owl is wise but the goose has genius.

A goose liver is not long for this world

You can't persuade a pigeon but you can force a goose.

Foie gras is French for butter.

Never butter a German's schnitzel.

Wiener schnitzel isn't a breed of dog.

A Dachshund makes a poor casserole.

A dog for Christmas should not take over your life.

A dog at Christmas pulls no crackers.

A cracker without cheese is like a dog without fleas.

A dog at Christmas cracks no nuts.

A Christmas dawg ain't so hot

One man's chipolata is another man's Frankfurter.

A Spanish Frank is not a sausage.

A Spaniard's sausage is easily sliced.

Barcelona is not in Spain.

A matador's cape is not fastened with Velcro.

A bull in the ring is like a sword in a sheath.

A bull in a china shop earns no loyalty points.

A Chinese Tesco's has no cat steak.

A Chinese cat sleeps in its slippers.

Foot binding is no friend to shoehorns.

A bound foot never oversteps the mark.

Pigeon toes do not tip.

A man who fancies pigeons has nothing to be ashamed of.

A pigeon with one leg is the victim of a crime.

There are no prosthetics for pigeons.

A pirate doesn't keep a pigeon.

A pirate's main brace is his own affair.

A beard without a moustache is an Amish crime.

A moustache without a beard belongs on a policeman.

A policeman is always ready to charge.

A laughing policeman is in the wrong job.

What is a policeman without his weapon?

Never trust a vicar with water cannon.

Never trust a soldier with a fire hose.

A sailor with a rubber duck sinks no ships.

A black rubber duck is no friend of baths.

A rubber chicken needs no basket.

A rubber chicken lays rubber eggs.

A rubber egg makes an everlasting omelette.

A rubber bullet never breaks the skin.

A skinhead doesn't need anti frizz serum.

A bald eagle is well feathered.

A bird in the hand is unhygienic.

An unwashed hand is a dangerous shake.

An unwashed sheikh is a dangerous friend.

A private jet is not for poets.

You won't find J.H. Prynne in a hot tub.

You won't find Mao in Cambridge.

Chairman Mao did not hold focus groups.

Chairman Mao loved men.

Chairman Mao never gave a massage.

A collarless jacket is no use for a tie.

Chairman Mao didn't wear a onesie.

One piece suits aren't just for bears and babies.

A man in a bear suit should not visit the zoo.

A baby boy in a bear suit is more than a man.

A boy in a suit has an elasticated tie.

A bear needs nowt but salmon and blueberries.

A bear with small hands catches no fish.

A bear with big teeth eats plenty of salmon

A lion doesn't need anger management.

A bear could take a lion in the woods.

A lion in the woods has a poor sense of self.

A bear in the savannah better find a tree.

A bear in a top hat is not always a magician.

A bear in a square is combing his hair.

Never high five a freemason.

Freemasons only control the country if you let them.

Freemasons don't get restraining orders.

Freemasons are hand shakers.

A joke about Quakers always involves oats.

Two biscuits in the hand are worth one in the mouth.

A Jaffa Cake isn't one of your five a day.

A Jaffa orange lives in fear of the sun.

An orange in one's pocket looks spectacular in jodhpurs.

An Oompa Loompa is not born orange.

Never take a dump in a chocolate factory.

Never mistake a dump for a chocolate factory.

A chocolate factory should not make fireguards.

Never trust a free ticket.

Never judge a man by his bus pass.

A bus pass is only as good as its picture

A gherkin in a lunchbox is a curious blessing.

A tram kills silently, a bus kills cyclists.

You can't win the Tour de France on a bike with a basket.

You can't win the Tour de France seven times without a little help.

Bradley Wiggins didn't invent sideburns.

Lance Armstrong didn't invent EPO.

Blood doping is best done after *Mastermind*.

The seven silvers will always be second.

A Uruguayan is always offside.

A German bowl is not for fruit.

You can't make *duck a l'orange* with a lemon.

You can't make San Pelligrino with chips.

You can't beat the system but you can batter a haddock.

A haddock is home in the water.

Never share your bath with a piranha.

Never Turk a bathhouse.

You don't have to bend over for a Turkish Delight.

A Turkish Delight is not a giant jelly tot.

There is no fun in a fun size Snickers.

A fun run is rarely so.

There is never a good enough reason to wear a tracksuit.

A shell suit pocket is made for fireworks.

You won't learn Latin from a Roman candle.

Rome wasn't built out of clay.

Caligula never got counselling.

Nero did not like coffee.

Marcus Aurelius didn't call customer services.

The Tao of Tom is not for kids.

Better a straw that bends than a swizzle stick.

Better a bamboo cane than an oak stick.

People who live with pandas should not build with bamboo.

A panda without bamboo is ever hungry.

Hungry snake make treacherous neck tie.

Hungry tie makes a man successful in business.

A bow tie does not a Chippendale make.

A male stripper is not always what he seems.

A man in a G-string does not know the whole alphabet.

A thong is not strapped for battle.

Never chew gum in Spearmint Rhino.

Never bring coins to a lady disco.

Never loosen your nuts at a roller disco.

A nut in the teeth is a friend to dentists.

A sabre toothed tiger eats no lettuce.

A tiger's friend is not his toothpick.

One man's toothpick is another man's crutch.

An insect's crutch is no higher than a toothpick.

A bee has no friends, just colleagues.

A bee sting is not just for Christmas.

Even bees don't listen to Sting.

Don't stand so, don't stand so, don't stand so close to me.

Never trust a white man singing reggae.

Never trust a whale with its mouth closed.

Only tuna should get friendly with dolphins.

One dolphin Jesus can forgive the Japanese.

If Jesus was a dolphin, he wouldn't jump through hoops.

If Jesus had a baby would it be potent?

Baby Bel will not save mankind.

A cheese has no parents.

Dutch babies are not born with rind.

Dutch poets are multi-lingual.

Belgian poets do not exist.

Belgian waffles are not for the light hearted.

You can't be brief in a waffle house.

A man must plough with such an ox as he has.

A pickled ploughman ploughs a wayward furrow.

A mill, a clock and a woman always want mending.

Time is an illusion, but lunch is at 12.

Choose a wife by your ear rather than your eye.

There's no point whispering in an echo chamber.

A growing youth has a wolf in his belly.

A wolf does not need slipper socks.

Green woods make a hot fire.

Green underpants are best left to elves.

He is like a hog, never good when living.

A handsome hostess is bad for the purse.

You can't fit a hostess in a hostess trolley.

An old man in a house is a good sign.

An old man in a greenhouse should not pass wind.

Wisdom prefers an unjust peace to a just war.

Norman Wisdom did not conquer England.

As busy as a hen with one chick.

As busy as a monkey in a nutcracker shop.

An egg in winter is always hard boiled.

Who can shave an egg?

A hairy egg makes hairy mayonnaise.

A hairy maze is hard to escape.

A hairy man is not always a werewolf.

It is hard for an empty bag to sit upright.

There is no need to frost a doughnut.

Insolence puts an end to friendship.

A showroom dummy makes a false friend.

Anthony Hopkins is master of puppets.

Never trust a puppet that can talk.

An egg without a beard is no Viking.

A Viking's smorgasbord is sacrosanct.

Fly agaric in the piss can only make for a fine warrior.

A samurai does not buy his sushi from Tesco.

Proper sushi is not made from chicken.

A chicken in a fish farm catches no salmon.

A butcher's dog has no dick.

A butcher's dog does not eat radishes.

A radish has no place in an abattoir.

A radish in a pew surprises the vicar.

A vicar without a collar is a human being.

You can't take an oath on a Kindle.

You can't take a Kindle seriously.

An Amazonian woman has delivery charges.

A giant anaconda is too long for love.

A python in one's trousers is a mixed blessing.

A snake's egg has no white.

A Creme Egg never hatches.

A Creme Egg is a seasonal food.

The Easter bunny makes a melancholy pie.

The rabbit is not a religious symbol.

Never lay straw in another man's hutch.

A straw hat will be ready to burn.

A scarecrow's hat needs no milliner.

Wurzel Gummidge is not a friend to crows.

You can't teach a crow humility.

You can't crow a teacher humbly.

A cheetah has no need for amphetamines.

A bad reading of Burgess is better than a good reading of McCabe.

A man in a bear skin needs no long johns.

A shaman has more in common with a bear than a man.

A shaman shouldn't claim expenses.

A shaman should be careful where he gardens.

Never leave soil on a lady's lettuce.

Never ingest unwashed greens.

A slug has no place in a lady's rockery.

A plug has no place in a lady's travel bag.

A gentleman's bum bag is his own affair.

A bag of cocks is not for sucking.

A rooster needs no wake up call.

A chicken is not an egg.

A cracked egg makes a poor paperweight.

An urn is more than a paperweight.

Never smoke an undertaker's roll up.

An undertaker today is a friend for tomorrow.

Never trust a man with a tape measure.

Trust a man who knows he's got a tapeworm.

You can't take a tapeworm for a walk.

You can tape a worm to the wall.

A worm shouldn't work in a spaghetti factory.

Earthworm Jim has come to save the day.

A worm that turns is still a worm.

A snake eating its own tail is hungry.

An lazy python is a draught excluder.

A python is not an anaconda.

Better Henry Fonda than an anaconda.

Better Jon Voight than Angelina Jolie.

Brad Pitt does not shell his own pistachios.

A raisin with nice teeth is still a dried grape.

A sultana is a disappointed grape.

A sultana does not rule the Ottoman Empire.

The Ottoman Empire never wins Eurovision.

The Ottoman Empire is not a sofa megastore.

In a world without armchairs, the leatherette pouffe is king.

The arms of a chairs are not for wrestling.

Never arm wrestle an onanist.

Onan was a lonely man.

Onan didn't need a vasectomy.

Conan liked to swing his sword.

Arnold Schwarzenegger doesn't wax his own legs.

Arnold Schwarzenegger is one of the greatest men alive.

Arnold Schwarzenegger has no need of Austria.

A man can govern a state he cannot pronounce.

Machiavelli didn't eat hummus.

A man is a wretched eel with legs.

A jellied eel makes a poor aquarium.

Jelly in the fish tank is not feeding fish.

You can't be a big shot in a Little Chef.

A happy fish is a ready dinner.

Never play Twister with an octopus.

Never eat a live octopus.

An octopus' embrace is meaningless.

An embrace of calamari is no more than a starter.

A squid ring is not a basis for a marriage.

A battered banana is not Chinese.

A battered banana is a small price for pleasure.

A pineapple fritter wastes its money.

A pineapple is not born with chunks.

A pineapple is born with a core.

A pink grapefruit deceives only fools.

A sour grapefruit is good for the arse.

One man's grapefruit is another man's gooseberry.

One grapefruit to many and you'll turn sour.

A peach fuzz need not be shaved.

A man who visits the barber more than once a month is vain.

Only a vain man has a mirror in the toilet.

Only a toilet has a mirror above the sink.

Never trust a man with a cracked sink.

Never crack a man with a sink.

Never trust a man with a sausage in his suitcase.

Never save money in a safe made of sausage.

Never be frank with a frankfurter.

Never onion a ring of fire.

An onion ring is not legally binding.

A wedding ring is not for life.

Wedding rings are best worn on fingers.

Rings of fire are best not walked through.

Johnny Cash didn't have a nectar card.

A nectar card is better than a Club Card.

Never place an unexpected item in the bagging area.

Never leave a bag unattended.

A battery hen is not rechargeable.

A Furby lives only within the Lithuanian borders.

A Furby makes a fickle friend.

A Furby is not a girlfriend.

You don't need a mortgage for a Wendy house.

You don't need Sylvanian Families to legalise gay marriage.

Sylvanian families shouldn't go to Center Parcs.

Sylvanian families should not holiday in northern Romania.

Never trust the woodland folk with toothpicks.

Never desolate Smaug.

Gandalf didn't use Lynx Africa.

Saruman never seemed to be a good wizard.

The eye of Sauron needs no contact lense.

The eye of Sauron looks like a bumhole.

Bilbo Baggins doesn't have an iPad.

Frodo Baggins was a lesser hobbit.

Gollum didn't have many friends on Facebook.

The Golem was originally Jewish.

You can't buy a Golem in Marks and Spencer.

You can't take a golem to a stag do.

The tooth fairy is never off with stress.

Dentists don't wear rubber trousers.

Never borrow Ken Dodd's toothbrush.

Never trust an ostrich with your accounts.

A good accountant makes a bad sexual partner.

A bad sexual partner is always accountable.

All is fair in love and sumo.

The sumo diet makes athletes fat.

Never let a sumo wrestler sit on your knee.

Never knee a samurai in the groin.

Samurai don't wear dressing gowns.

Samurai sharpen their swords on peasants.

Never ask a samurai to segment your grapefruit.

A grapefruit needs no seeds to bloom.

The Duke of Wellington didn't drink chai latte.

Napoleon wasn't abnormally short.

Admiral Nelson didn't eat quinoa.

Keenwah is not an insulation material.

You can't woo a lady with couscous.

Gaunt couscous makes for a drab salad.

Better a limp lettuce than a frozen radish.

Don't soak lettuce in a tuna's brine.

Dolphins are intelligent, but they can't do Sudoku.

Maths is for the sea.

An octopus can only count up to eight.

An orca counts only for limbs of Man.

You can take a panda to Edinburgh, but you can't make it mate.

A panda is good on the eyes but not on the nose.

A panda has no use for mascara.

A panda is a picky eater.

People who live with pandas shouldn't install a separate toilet.

A starved panda is no use to anyone.

A hungry panda ruins the reception.

A hungry reception is ready for anything

A drunk monk wears no cassock.

A cassock is not a deep sea fish.

Better a Cossack in your cassock than a rabbit in your habit.

There ain't many Jews left on the Volga.

Never touch a Rabbi's matzo balls.

A cake is never kosher.

A fishcake needs no candles.

A cake candle is lit by fish.

An underwater candle is but the dream of a mermaid.

A mermaids dream is to have a reproductive system.

A mermaid needs no cobbler.

A little mermaid would simply not survive in the ocean.

A little mermaid needs barely a crab stick.

A crab stick is made of fish parts.

One man's crab stick is another's Excalibur.

One crab stuck is another crab free.

A lobster doesn't have anyone on speed dial.

A lobster in the pot is worth two in the bush.

Never argue with a lobster naked.

A rubber band is a lobster's muzzle.

A rubber band is as good as a mistress.

A coil is not always twisted.

A snake does not belong in a sock drawer.

A sock is not a tissue.

A shoe for business, a slipper for pleasure.

A slipper is an open question.

A gentleman's slipper is always tartan.

A tartan flash is always welcome.

A man in a kilt should learn to cross his legs.

A skirt is not good for battle.

Vikings didn't have meditation workshops.

Vikings go to Valhalla.

You never see a Viking in Argos.

You'll never see a Viking crying.

You can't pillage in a pullover.

The Blue nun welcomes the coming Viking.

Sister Wendy doesn't cull badgers.

A badger is best left alone.

A badger makes a poor partner for bridge.

A bridge too far is a bridge too many.

A troll without Twitter had best stick to goats.

A tweet without a troll is a sound unheard.

A bird in the hand is unhygienic.

A bird in the groin is painful.

The early bird is easily tired.

The Chinese dragon is all you can eat.

A Chinese burn isn't always a race crime.

A race to Beijing is always well attended.

A Peking duck doesn't want your crusts.

A crispy duck won't quack.

What's sauce for the goose is only available in Waitrose.

He who shops in Waitrose shops short-sighted.

Aldi and Lidl were not Norse gods.

Freya is a name both middle class and old school.

The Hammer of the Gods isn't sold in B & Q.

The hammer of Thor is not a boomerang.

Never touch the tools in Odin's shed.

A crow to Odin is a liver to kidneys.

Blackbirds in a pie is against the law.

A beak in a berry is a wise beak.

A seagull in the living room spoils Strictly Come Dancing.

Baking soda is a seagull's poison.

A snooker ball has no place in a fruit bowl.

A snooker referee must wear a waistcoat.

A man in a waistcoat isn't necessarily a waiter.

An old waiter is French.

A French polisher need be neither French, nor Polish.

A Polish shop is sklep.

A Frenchman doesn't always know his onions.

A French onion soup is fresh in France.

A Frenchman's onions gather no moss.

A kidney stone is not fun to pass.

A kidney stone does not a rockery make.

A bleeding urethra needs know no more rocks.

A fool and his gherkins are soon pickled.

A gherkin is not a pickle.

You can't go to sea in a gravy boat.

A poet writing proverbs is not a poet.

A poet writing proverbs is worth two in the bush.

www.ingramcontent.com/pod-product-compliance
Lightning Source LLC
Chambersburg PA
CBHW022125040426
42450CB00006B/849